"I guess this is the book that I should have read a more than 20 years ago! I suppose it is never too late, so I'll see where it takes me from here!"

- Rolf Stange

Author of "Spitsbergen-Svalbard", which over more than 15 years has developed into a widely used standard guidebook, and numerous other books on Svalbard, Bear Island, Jan Mayen and Greenland

www.spitsbergen-svalbard.com

"When I first heard about Polar Permaculture I was amazed. Growing food inside the Arctic Circle sounded like the hardest thing ever to do. And yet, undaunted, Benjamin went ahead and did just that! In his book you'll get to learn the secrets of what drove him to succeed and how you can do the same for yourself. Setting up my own business was the best thing I ever did. If I'd had a copy of this book back then I imagine it would've helped me no end. Best wishes,"

-Aranya Austin, Permaculture teacher, designer and author

www.learnpermaculture.com

My name is Thomas-and I have both worked and travelled in the Arctic for 25 years. First in Greenland where I worked,and then as a visitor on Svalbard in March 2004.

After reading Benjamin Vidmar's book-I was both deeply touched and also inspired by his commitment and enthusiasm to his vision and project to Polar Permaculture on Svalbard. It is this commitment that also made his own Country put a man on the Moon.

I know how harsh and difficult the life in The Arctic is-so I can only say that I deeply respect Benjamin for his work up there-but sadly some people did their best to make his dream not come true..

I hope that this book will maybe inspire others to make their own vision come true.

Thomas Below - Arctic Traveller from Copenhagen,Denmark...

**Thomas with his rifle
at Barentsburg,
Svalbard**
Thomas Below

Thinking of starting up your own business? You need to read this book first!

Starting a business can be filled with unexpected pitfalls —one author seeks to offer advice for any fledging entrepreneur.

When author Benjamin L. Vidmar wanted to start up a permaculture business near the North Pole, he was met with assurances that he was going to fail. After all, he was attempting the impossible. Or was he?

His business boomed until COVID-19. Now he's here to share the 10 steps he used to do the impossible.

You'll learn:

- · 10 Real steps to take for success
- · That you're responsible for your success
- · The impossible is possible
- · To dig deep and bring out the winner in you
- · Lessons in failure
- · ...and so much more!

Knowledge is essential in any startup. Arm yourself with the same knowledge one man used to do the impossible and set yourself up for success. Whether you're considering starting a business, are in the process, are already established, or are struggling, this book can help you. You hold the power to change your life; scroll up and one-click buy your copy now!

PRAISE FOR CHEW ON THIS!

"I first heard about Polar Permaculture in a report on icepeople.net. I was immediately fascinated by this project. Ben spent years chasing his dream on the edge of the world. Although Polar Permaculture didn't eventually come to fruition due to bad luck, Ben had learned a lot along the way and shared it with us in this book."
- Chun at 78°N@satofishi

"Benjamin Vidmar is one of the greatest minds among American expats. Few have dared to jump into the unknown as he has. If you are in need of motivation and inspiration on your entrepreneurial journey, or if you need a dose of focus in your life, then this book is for you."
- John Alan Reese, creator of the popular podcast "The Comin' Home Podcast With John Alan", radio program creator and producer, writer, coach

www.johnalanpod.com

CHEW ON THIS!

BENJAMIN L. VIDMAR

CHEW ON THIS!

ARCTIC FOOD FOR THOUGHT AND LESSONS FOR SUCCESS

Polar Permaculture LLC

FOREWORDS FROM MY FIRST MENTORS

Doing the impossible is something that great people view as a challenge. Benjamin L. Vidmar is an international chef, adventurer, entrepreneur and permaculture expert. He has traveled the world in his learning journey and has found his purpose on the top of the world. Chew on this! Arctic food for thought and lessons for success, offers the reader ten empowering steps to achieve the impossible. It is a testament to what is doable when you remove the limitations, both internal and external. Ben's journey has allowed him to circle the globe and embrace a multitude of cultures. It has helped him to live life, without the traditional constrictions and boundaries that prevent most people from attaining greatness.

Chew On This teaches that freedom embraced is freedom achieved. It offers an encouraging message for those who are seeking purpose in a world rife with duplication and imitation. Vidmar's story teaches us to focus our attention on who and what we are chosen to be. It is a tale of courage, fortitude and dedication to a vision.

We need more stories like Chew on this! Arctic food for thought and lessons for success and we need more individuals like Benjamin L. Vidmar, people who are willing to risk everything for the vision that has been placed before them and the purpose that beckons them onward.

Paul Hobson Sadler, Sr.

I have worked in the food and beverage business for over 40 years. Having had the privilege of working
with many bright and ambitious culinarians throughout this career, Benjamin Vidmar to this day remains
one of a kind. I have never worked with anyone as driven and ambitious as Ben. From the first day I met
him, I could tell this man was different. His passion for food, the industry, and his constant growth as
professional and person was unlike anyone I have ever met before. Like a thirst that could not be
quenched coupled with a free spirit that was going to go and conquer wherever the wind would take
him.
 When you read his book, you can sense his rapid-fire relentless thought process and his nonstop
commitment to being the best at what he does and achieving his goals. Yes, there are many books on
the topic of how to set goals and achieve them. I can assure you though this one was written by a man
with blood, sweat, and dirt under his nails, along with a resume that includes successful growing
vegetables on a frozen rock at edge of the world.
 Your #1 fan Ben!

Chef Jim Gelzheiser

I would like to dedicate this book to everyone who has helped, volunteered, interned, thought about, reached out to us, taken a tour, interviewed or been part of Polar Permaculture Solutions, AS in any shape or form.

You know who are you, and none of this would have been possible without your support. I would also like to thank my family who have stood by me during the entire process as I used time, energy, and money to plan, grow, and develop the company in Longyearbyen.

None of this would have been possible without the commitment of Elena, Amir-Soffian, Laila-Rheanna, Alif-Ikhwan, Vlasa Benjamina, Mira Benjamina, Fluffy and Ferarri.

I would also like to give a special thanks to my two greatest heroes:

Mia, my mother and Kathrine, my grandmother, who both worked hard, ate well, and made me into the man I am today.

I hope you benefit from my experience and achieve all of your dreams!

CONTENTS

CONTENTS

INTRODUCTION

Are you interested in starting your own business or working for yourself? I have always had a passion for cooking, but did not take it seriously enough in the beginning. Have you felt pressure from society to be something you are not or do something that you do not want to do? I felt huge pressure to go to university and to get a college degree, but I never enjoyed being in class or sitting for exams. I prefer to work with my hands, and there is definitely a need for more people with skills these days. In this book, I will try to take you on a journey that I have been living for the last twelve years of my life near the north pole. Svalbard is an amazing place and I highly recommend you to visit it if you have a chance. Longyearbyen is the largest city there and it is where I found myself working as a chef for a few years. The amazing thing about Svalbard is that people must decide to be there and will only stay if they like it. Of course in other cities people have an option to leave if they want, but I have never been to a place where you either love it or hate it. No one tolerates Svalbard like people do in a normal city, and it creates a unique bond between all of the individuals living there.

Svalbard is part of Norway, but the city of Longyearbyen was actually founded by an American businessman, John Munro Longyear back in 1905. This has also inspired me while I was there and got me thinking about how I could contribute to making the place better. I wanted to green the place and I re-membered telling a group of people this way before I got the idea to start producing food. Since I worked in all of the restaurants in town, I had my finger on the pulse of what was happening in regards to the freshness and quality of food being delivered. It was expensive and difficult to get locally grown produce, so I decided to grow my own.

In this book, I will attempt to tell my story and share some of the lessons I have learned from this journey that I have been on for so many years. I am in a unique position to show you how to make the impossible possible, and if I can do this, then so can you. Whatever it is that you desire is within your reach and the first step to obtaining it is to create a burning desire for it. What would you do if you never had to worry about money? What is your passion? What do you love? What makes you happy? I would like you to keep these questions in mind as you take this journey with me and I shed light on some of the lessons I have learned.

I wish you success and luck on your adventure before, during, and after you have read this book. The point of this is to focus on yourself and your story. Please use what I say here to your benefit and continue to follow your dreams. I will see you at the top and just let me know if you have any questions or concerns.

THE SKY'S THE LIMIT

Stay far from timid, only make moves
when you're heart's in it, and live the phrase
the sky's the limit. - The Notorious B.I.G.

If you are going to set yourself up for success in life, then you need to set some meaningful goals for yourself. First things first, a positive attitude is the most important ingredient for success. Yes, it is! As you come closer to achieving your goal, you will discover it is all about your attitude. Attitude covers how you act and react to things and people around you. A positive attitude, no matter the situation, will set you up for the success you seek in any goal you set.

One of the winning strategies to keeping a positive

attitude I have discovered: You can always find the opportunities in any failed endeavor or barrier for example, when I lost my company on Svalbard during a bankruptcy, I thought it was the end of the world and I went into a huge depression that lasted for months. I just could not understand why this was happening to me and how to get myself out of the funk. The press had a field day with it and everyone has blamed me for things beyond my control. This is a horrible experience, but all is not lost because of the contacts that I have made and the lessons I have learned. Covid-19 caused our town's tourism industry to grind to a halt which resulted in me losing all potential earnings for 2021 which led to a domino effect. I declared bankruptcy back in June of 2021, but that is not the end of my story or of this adventure.

Before Covid-19, I was in a unique situation running one of the most innovative companies in the "northernmost" town in the world, Longyearbyen. After this two year period of struggling and finally getting back on my feet, I have come to realize it was necessary for me to move on and leave that place. Everything was difficult to implement there in Longyearbyen, and I was getting accustomed to all of the resistance and embracing it. This was counterproductive for the business, but it did help for me to develop determination and extremely tough skin. I could not have imagined two years ago, when everything was going so badly, that I would actually be in the situation I am now. Now I am in a location that is much more conducive to what I want to do and it is much easier to get things done.

Get out of your comfort zone, rediscover yourself for a more fulfilling offer, go to a passion you had previously put aside, or maybe even start your own business. Of course, maintaining a positive attitude does not negate the existence of what I felt at the time I lost my company, but by looking at the situation differently, I was able to create other feelings that helped to propel me further. Hence, rather than wallow negatively in a situation that is out of my control, I instead took charge and moved with the energy to redefine the story.

Another strategy is to surround yourself with a network of positive people. They will keep you sane! We are mostly a sum of the people we surround ourselves with. Our immediate network influences us in ways we cannot even imagine. How well do you know those in your close network? Who is your source of inspiration/motivation? Who do you spend more time with? These point to your immediate network. To surround yourself with a network of positive people, you will need to be deliberate about who you let into your space. So, there are many ways to attain the positive attitude that keeps you charging towards your goal no matter the circumstances.

Failing once is not the end of you, or the story. If you get turned down once, stay positive and tell yourself, "I did not come so far, to only come this far". No one has reached success without falling a few times and getting some bruises along the way. If others can deal with this and continue to fight for success, then so can you. These may seem like just mere words, but only to an individual who is not prepared to leave their comfort zone. The least you can do for yourself is to not settle with failing or allowing it to define who you are. You are not what happens to you. However, your reactions can define or redefine who you are. Get a grip on your life and drive it regardless of the barrier of failing at one or more things. The goal is to enjoy the process while reaching for the skies and do not get caught up in the fear of failing.

Reach for the Moon and
if you miss, you will
still be covered in
Stardust

It is better to aim too high, even if you do not succeed in the beginning. Aiming high allows you to dream big and shows you are more capable than you realize. When you do only what you think is possible, you limit your possibilities and lower your true standards. The problem with lower standards of yourself is that you lower your aim and confine yourself. We many times ask the universe for things, and when the universe seeks to provide what we ask, we turn away and quit. There is no way to get what you want without a test of your will and of your abilities. The more chances you test your will and abilities, then the more likely you are to receive what your heart desires.

Have you asked yourself what the habits of the most successful people you know are? You do not even have to look far, just look around you. You will surely find a few successful individuals you can observe and note what makes them successful. One of such is their habits, what they consider a routine. Habits, for many people, can seem micro to being successful, but habits make a big difference. It is the making of an individual. Hence, to aim high, you must first develop habits that keep you grounded in the face of any circumstances, good or bad.

Another thing to consider is that aiming high might really look vague to those who have not learned the act of visualization. I mean, this is not that they do not have big dreams, they only have a problem visualizing them. Hence, there is a need to break the big goal into smaller goals. Indeed, the colossal success we hope to achieve is an accumulation of several minor achievements. So, take care of the minor achievements and keep climbing until the sky is within your reach.

Long-term goals or dreams that take a while to come into reality can be tiring. Sometimes, quitting appears as a more profitable option, as keeping at it can feel like a waste of time and other resources. Times like this call for evaluation, and this is core to success. It is important that you track how far you have come. This process will help set a better perspective than just taking an irrational decision to quit. Many do not consider quitting to be an option at all, but this type of mentality can come with a lot of tension which can make one go to any length (even illegally) to win. I would rather one see quitting as not an option until it is the only option. This can only happen when a thorough evaluation of oneself and the process up to where one is has been revised.

Goals cannot achieve themselves outside of your capacity. The beauty of focusing your success on the journey is that you get to value the capacity built as you climb up. Even when quitting presents itself as the only option, you will discover you will have developed more than you could have imagined. Your self-improvement is key to aiming high and reaching for the skies.

One of the main reasons this does not happen is because of self-doubt and fear of failure. We all know that sick feeling of doubt. It is super uncomfortable to think that maybe you made a mistake by investing in yourself. It is uncomfortable to admit that you do not trust yourself enough to take advantage of an opportunity. The thing about doubt is that it is always telling you something. Do not be quick to discard your doubt and fears. See them as doorways to walk through.

Your downfall begins and your dreams seem more unattainable when you accept your fears and self-doubt. Ask yourself this; what do you stand to lose by aiming higher and pushing yourself further? You may miss at first or you may reach your dream on the first try. How will you know unless you give it your best shot? Take a chance and jump full speed into your destiny. The higher your aim, the more you can achieve. Even if you do not reach your goal or fall short, you will not end up so far away from it. And even more promising is that even if you miss the sky, you are still the champion who aimed at it, and you cannot be where you used to be regarding your personal development.

Being humble

It is necessary to be humble and to take advice when offered. I know how easy it is to think we know everything, but we miss so much when we shut down our feedback mechanism. Feedback is what it takes to get better and better. No one does things perfectly the first time, and it takes much practice to reach your goals. To learn from others' mistakes is where the fun truly is and learn with others' money when possible. I have made so many of my own mistakes and have done things the hard way, and to my detriment, but far more to my benefit.

There is this quote you may have heard before which states that "None of us is as smart as all of us. " by Kenneth Blanchard. This, for me, is the perfect expression of why we ought to humble ourselves and learn from other people. Sometimes, you may just not be aiming at the mark to make a decision that brings you to a better place. When you humble yourself to learn from others, what you do in that process is you welcome diverse social interactions. In times like those where you do not feel mentally capable of bringing yourself up, you can draw strength from these associations. It is a very healthy way of socializing as those giving their strength and support also feel closer to you. These sets of people are those who have passed through what we are currently going through, and, in other cases, they are just people who have enough experience to come up with a way out or options for you to pick from. Having such companions in your life is priceless, but only with humility can you find and keep such people.

Speaking about my mistakes, I usually would not be bothered to see what others had done in similar situations. During my years on Svalbard, I usually just did my own way without checking what others were working on. It makes sense to investigate what is happening around you in order to have a better understanding of the whole situation. If you have a great recipe for bread that was passed down through your family, then why would you throw it out and start from scratch? Of course, that is where the creativity comes from, but that recipe has been in your family for so many years for a reason, we must acknowledge its worth. Now when I meet new people, I always try to find out what this person's passion is and then I ask questions. These encounters are like mining and finding gold.

Set Goals you are passionate about

When setting goals, try to focus on how you really feel about them before you act on them. Think about how to achieve them, how it makes you feel and how much time you need to reach them. Your driving force will come from the fact that these goals make you feel a kind of way, and it will be much easier to reach if there are emotions involved. Ask yourself the following questions and see how they resonate with you:

- Why is this important to me?
- How does it make me feel?
- What am I willing to give to make this happen?

Setting goals is a vital part of the journey. Goal setting helps to add focus to your effort. As you go about doing your daily activities, you drive a lot of effort into those tasks to see that you accomplish them. There is no bigger picture of the effort you are putting in place, hence you will only have a disjointed and confusing pattern when analyzing your activities. No precision or concise pathway, just stuff being done with no direction or directive. Setting goals also helps measure your progress. It can be hard keeping track, but when you have where all your activities are supposed to lead to, then you can measure how far you have come, what needs to be done, how fast you have come and so on. It can be very easy to get discouraged when working towards success, because there is no measure to tell you have arrived unless you reach the goal.

There is a destination! When you know where you are headed, you can strategize how to get there. This feeling, when mixed with the original feeling of pursuing a goal you feel most connected to, can be the right motivation that will keep you going until you accomplish your goal. Then there is the enormous pressure and reality of procrastinating. You may deal with such challenges as part of your goals by creating a timeline and benchmarks for completion.

Setting goals might seem easy, but following through is usually where the trouble develops and also the complications. As I write this, it is the second day of 2022, and I am sure that many of you have set New Year's resolutions after that doozie of the year 2021. Now I will ask you this, how many of you have kept those resolutions until now? Many of us have done this for so long that it has now become a habit, but what if we all stopped to think and ask the following question: Why? Without passion and driving force behind our wishes, they soon become memories until repeated the next time.

The most important aspect of this process is to not only set goals, but to set passionate, purpose driven goals instead.

Do you believe in yourself?

If you do not, then how can you expect others to believe in you? Self-doubt has a way of creeping in and paralyzing my performance, especially when I am doing something that I am not comfortable with. When I first started Polar Permaculture, I knew what I wanted, but did not know how to get it done. I was usually waiting for someone to come and help me, but that is never the case.

Why was it so difficult for me to find the courage to believe in myself and my abilities? I was so busy second guessing myself and the mission. My dream was to make Svalbard green and to have local food there on the island. Everything was imported from the mainland, and we only had a few local resources: fish, reindeer, birds, and some mushrooms. There are not enough reindeer for everyone to eat locally, so most of the reindeer we eat are imported from Scandinavia. What about the fish? Why do we not eat more local fish instead of importing frozen fish? Well, this is complicated because there is no regulated fishing industry on Svalbard. They have been working for the last few years to set up a fishing industry, but it has not been done by the time I left the island during May 2021.

I have never eaten frozen fish in my life until I started

working on the ships traversing the Polar Regions. Before that, we only ate fresh fish, and it spoiled me in that regard. It is common on Svalbard to eat frozen fish, and when there is fresh fish once a week at the local grocery store, you can imagine the price would be higher than the price of buying the frozen fish. We just accepted this as part of life when we all live in the "northernmost" town in the world, Longyearbyen.

I could not accept it, and this was exactly the main reason I set up Polar Permaculture to grow food in town and share it with others. Many thought I was crazy for wanting to attempt such a feat. This is usually something that the government, universities, or larger companies take responsibility for, but this was not the case on Svalbard. Many universities have done experiments with flowers in Longyearbyen, and there was some agriculture production in the Russian settlements, but not so much in the Norwegian part of the islands. This is an example of the hardships that I faced and how I dealt with them. I never gave up, which is why I did not fail and WHY I had to succeed. I know if I can do it, then so can you!

Set a date and stick to it

Goals without an end date are much more difficult to reach. Without setting a time frame, there will be no sense of urgency or pressure to make it happen. Getting things done is amazing, but the added pressure of getting it done on time is even better! By setting a deadline for a specific task, you will make yourself more productive and work more efficiently. Giving yourself 24 hours to complete a specific task means you need to prioritize it and focus your energy. Those 24 hours will be used in the most productive manner possible. If you were to change the deadline for the same task to say, for example, one week, this would totally change the way you approach the task entirely. Just think about it like this: how much time would be wasted taking one week to do a task that can be done in 24 hours? I am sure you have experience with this, and the most important lesson here is to push yourself.

The time frame you choose must be realistic and attainable if you are to accomplish it and reach your goals. Traveling the world in one day? Not possible, not attainable, and not worth it even if you could. How much would you truly get to experience if you only had one day to travel the world? Giving yourself one year to travel the world would totally open up more opportunities now, would it not? Use your gut and your heart when deciding on a time frame for your goals. It is important to understand the goal and how you feel about it personally. The stronger you feel about it, the easier it will be for you to allocate time each day to get it done.

Never surrender

Giving up is a state of mind, and you can lose without surrendering. "Never surrender" is my motto and I always try to find the silver lining in any situation. I remember when we hatched quails on Svalbard. It is illegal to import agriculture birds, and to do agriculture on Svalbard, because of issues with safety. I received some fertilized eggs from a farmer in Stavanger, and the eggs came through the post with no issues. If I would have just eaten those eggs, then there would never have been any issues, but I hatched them to see what it was like to have chicks. I did not have any experience with this, and it was always my dream to have my own eggs from my own birds.

By this time, Polar Permaculture was producing some microgreens and leafy greens, but our location was so small, and it was nearly impossible to get a larger location. We had been discussing with all organizations that would have options for a new location, but there was nothing of worth. It was extremely expensive to run this business, and I was always looking for ways to earn more. With about 80 birds, I was producing around 50 eggs per day and could sell one egg for about 5nok (\$,50). Everyone wanted to buy our eggs, and it finally felt like things would turn around. The health department was not happy about me producing eggs and forced me to kill all of my birds. I was upset and fought for as long as I could, but I eventually had to kill all of my birds and was deeply wounded from the experience. Since the company started, most of the money came from tourism, and we were running different tours to meet our budget.

MAKE YOUR DECISION

Those who reach decisions promptly and definitely, know what they want, and generally get it. - Napoleon Hill

Life is all about the decisions we make every day. Many of those decisions are so small we do not even think about it, but others are big, with profound implications for our lives. Most times, the decisions we make affect other people's lives, hence the need to be careful and not just decide impulsively. Making moral decisions involves you investigating the situation. After you have thoroughly considered the options available, then you can settle with a decision that will be final. Any process that presses you for an instant decision might not be ideal.

The most important thing to remember above all is to evaluate all aspects of an issue before deciding anything about it. When you decide, the path reveals itself to you. I grew my food after much hesitation and doubt from myself. Being from Florida, I was just planning to spend a season or two on the island, and then eventually go back home to grow and work with Permaculture principles. There were no projects on the island, and most who came were more concerned about going out in nature than where our food was sourced.

Growing Near the North Pole

The decision to grow food in such a remote location was difficult to make, but I stuck with it after the decision was made, no matter what happened. What is the point of growing vegetables on Svalbard if everything is imported? I can remember how difficult it was to get the supplies and how many mistakes I made to get things right. I was never afraid of making those mistakes and have learned so much from the process. Luckily, Svalbard is a tax-free zone, and this allowed me to order supplies from everywhere I wanted without VAT (TAX) issues. Sometimes I think it would have been better to pay the important tax if I could have gotten a cheaper transport cost. Transport cost to Svalbard can range any-where from 20 to 40% of the total cost.

My decision to make Svalbard green has been an inspiration to many others around the world that have reached out to me and shared their thoughts. How could my experience in such a small place have positively affected so many others around the world? If I had de-cided not to implement the project and return home to Florida, how different would have things been? I cannot even imagine not having started Polar Permaculture in Longyearbyen. It was like getting a PhD in life, and I have learned so much from that decision to do the project.

There have been people from all over the world visit-ing Svalbard and working with us to make this impos-sible mission possible. I could not have done it without the help of many interns, volunteers, supporters, part-ners, staff, family, and friends. The choices we make get us where we are. Look at where you want to be and make choices that lead in that direction. I found out that it is never a straight line and have tried to make the most of the journey. Sometimes the journey is more important than the destination, but it would never happen unless we make a choice. Choose now, and the path will be revealed!

Make Smarter Decisions

The little decisions we make daily in our lives are extremely important when you look at the big picture of everything. When you decide, it sets events forward in your life that can amount to something being good or bad for you. The smarter your decisions are, the more likely it will be rewarded with good. Making smarter decisions means doing what is right for you, and not based on what others want us to do. The people around you have an influence on you and that is why it is important to surround yourself with the people doing what you want to do.

You are the sum of the five people you associate yourself with daily. Who are you spending your time with now and what are they doing? Are they going the direction you want to go and doing things you want to do? If not, perhaps it is best if you spend more time around those who are and create a positive environment for you to accomplish your goals.

There is no one size fits all for making smarter decisions. It varies from person to person and usually involves feelings and emotions. For some people, their gut plays a role in making the best decision. This usually means that their first thought is the best thought for them. Overthinking the issue usually results in them making a bigger deal than necessary and making unnecessary decisions. For others, it is important to think about the options and make sure they have everything covered before deciding.

However, you like to decide, make sure you see things from as many perspectives as possible. Making smarter decisions will improve your quality of life and make things easier for you. The most important thing to remember is to not decide in haste or without proper knowledge. Once you have decided, then it is time to act, but do not rush to decide until it feels right to you.

Imagination Is Key

Everything that exists is created in the imagination first, before being transformed into the material world. Your mind is a lot more powerful than you think. It can imagine and trigger a visualization process that prompts you towards your new realities. Being able to think and come up with new ideas that could birth new realities was key for my survival on Svalbard. My first time on the island was in 2007. I worked on one of the expedition cruise ships going around the island. Working as head chef, I had an assistant in the galley with me to prepare food for 50 passengers. The company that ran the tours would sub-charter the ships from Russian research institutes, which meant that the crew were Russian and had full responsibility for the ship.

They had a chef who prepared food for the crew and all the crew had safety responsibilities on the ship. How was it possible for me to find a position like this with no sailor training? Well, as a passenger on the manifest, the small international team was only responsible for the comforts of the guests. Many would look at such a situation and say that because they do not have the proper training, they cannot work on the ship. I, however, looked at the situation and said to myself, how can I get a position like this and get paid to travel the world? It was an amazing experience, and the position paid in US dollars.

We also got tips, which meant that my salary was directly deposited into my bank account, and it was possible to survive on the tips when we made calls to different ports. I have always wanted to travel the world, but this usually required me spending money, time, and energy to make it happen. Now I was getting paid to travel the world, and all my flights were covered as well. When I first applied for this position, I never thought I would get it or that it was even true when they contacted me about the position.

The woman that interviewed me called and said she was representing the company, and that they were interested in my resume. She asked a few questions, and I also asked a few questions. We spoke for only about 30 mins, and she said that she liked what she heard. She also asked me if I wanted to be head chef or sous chef. I thought about it for a minute and asked to be the head chef. I was hired and they would send me tickets and all details in an email soon. This must be a joke, I told myself, but it was no joke. A few days later, I received all the details in an email and was soon on my way to Antarctica for the first time.

Implementing your Decisions

The decision process must end in action! Many people decide about the changes they want to manifest into their lives, but often end up neglecting them. Action is required to bring your decision to life and make it possible. Having passion, strong willpower, thick skin, and dedication about something will surely allow it to happen. If you do not take those first steps, whatever decision you make will just lie dormant and not give you the desired change you seek.

Think about the last decision you made, and if anything happened before you acted. A decision to learn how to drive a car is not the same as the actual stepping out to get someone that would teach you how to drive. However small your action seems; it is significantly better than just wishing your decision could implement itself. The conceptualization process is a vital part, but nothing really happens until you act on your words and thoughts. Remember that we are a product of our habits. If success is a desire, then you must develop habits that correspond to you becoming successful, hence the need for you to implement your decisions. Habits do not form on their own, they become through repeated actions. Sometimes you may not trace the decision you made that led you to where you are, but you can through looking at your implementation process. So, you see a lot of it hinges on you implementing those decisions.

Living on the edge

Svalbard literally translates to "the cold edge" and you can totally feel it after living there for some years. Yes, there are direct flights to Tromsø and Oslo, but being there feels like being on the edge of civilization. The satellites that orbit the Polar Regions are closer than traveling to Oslo. The internet connection there is extremely quick because of the two huge fiber optic cables that are connected to mainland Norway. I feel these are exactly the reasons that make the place so dynamic and interesting.

There are a few Facebook groups where you can easily see this magic in action. Say you have just arrived and accidentally leave your wallet and phone in the taxi. Well, this would promptly be transferred to the hotel you are staying with a note to give it back to you. If you lost something on the ground and someone found it, they would post it in the Facebook groups and suggest a way to give it back to you. I have not noticed this before in other places and I have never lived in a city where everyone wants to be there. It creates such a positive energy and environment that makes for a pleasant experience. The edge is where the most magic happens in nature, and I hope you agree that living on the edge is an experience that should not be missed.

No Regrets

If it was easy, then everyone would do it! This is something I reminded myself about many times while I was working to grow food near the North Pole. There will always be hurdles along the way and things you need to overcome to reach your goals. If you have passion before you make your decisions, then it should be easy to follow through and get what you want. Anytime you feel like quitting when things get difficult, just remember why you started it in the first place and have a laugh. Laughing is much easier to do than crying and will make you smile in the end. Focus your energy on the things you want and the things that make you feel good. Your time is valuable, and it is also super important to plan your time well and fight laziness as much as possible. Being lazy will stop you from doing things that are good for you. If you make mistakes, then it is not the end of the world you know? Make amends and carry on until you reach the top. Start making smarter decisions and do not wait for anyone. There is no hero coming to rescue you or to tell you how to do it. Let's go now! I will see you at the top of the mountain as I am waiting there for you, dear friend.

Speak Your Mind

From 2020 on, the situation with Polar Permaculture was becoming impossible to maintain and things were getting more complicated. One thing that I can say for sure during this mission to do the impossible was that I always felt free to speak my mind and try out new ideas. Everyone is usually used to doing things a certain way and not open to trying new things, but this is exactly how I could progress so much with my mission. I do not mean you need to be sassy and tell everyone off, but let people know where you stand on issues. As I was further developing the company and looking for oppor-tunities to expand, many people would come to me with different ideas, but it is impossible to do everything at once. I had to make it clear what my objectives were and to let people know what I wanted to focus on. The decision was up to me, and that meant I needed to stand my ground. I am a naturally shy person, so it is difficult for me to be in that role, but it is necessary to continue developing the impossible.

Focus your energy

Energy is the currency of the universe and what we must use to get what we want. We are always trading our energy for the things we want and need, and we are giving a certain amount of time to do this. A major challenge for me was learning how to control my energy and how to sharpen it like a laser. It will be impossible to achieve the impossible unless you can focus your energy into a laser beam of desire. For many years, I could not focus my energy, and I reaped no results. The moment I could concentrate and focus on my energy was when I found a great mentor, Hege. After that, I could take the company from a minus to a plus within one year. 2019 was the best year I had with Polar Permaculture and things were finally making sense as I was wrapping up the northern lights season leading into February 2020. From that point on, it did not matter how much I concentrated my energy because the entire island was shutting down for tourists because of the Covid-19 pandemic. This was the point of no return, and an extremely deep hole was created that was not possible to climb out of unfortunately.

LITTLE BY LITTLE

Focus on one thing, make it your priority, and stick with it no matter what! - Tyler Perry

There is a beautiful saying in Malay that I love so much and want to share with you: Sikit-Sikit Lama-Lama Jadi Bukit, which literally translates to, little by little -eventually you build a mountain. Look at the tallest mountains and imagine them when they first formed. Do you think they were as tall as they are now? You can become as successful as you want, but it will take time and energy. Going to the gym is a splendid example. You walk into the gym and immediately you see people just like you, but only differ in that they have the body type you desire. There is a common word used in the gym and it is called endurance, which reveals the need to keep at something even if you have not seen the result you want. The folks at the gym know you do not just walk in and walk out the same day with the results you want. These individuals understand the need to commit their time, energy to getting the result they want in life. And even if they do not see the immediate effect of their investment, they keep at it.

Be committed and persevere

Perseverance means having unwavering persistence in accomplishing anything, no matter how difficult it is or how many obstacles you encounter along the way. When working with a jigsaw puzzle, one technique I like to do is when one piece does not fit, I try another and build up the borders first. This is easiest for me, and I also carry it over to my daily life when working with my goals and success. It is most important to stay committed and persevere until you get what you want. By pushing yourself to be patient and stay committed, you have a much better chance of reaching your destination and getting your success. The key is to value the journey and not to be too concerned with the destination.

If I regret anything from my experience, it would be not being present more when things were happening. You can never go back, and soon it all becomes a memory. I have learned from my failures and did not fear them because, in hindsight; it was all necessary for me to get where I am now. Everything in life requires this kind of investment, from a successful business to personal relationships.

Have a Success Routine

We are all creatures of habits, and these habits help to shape our routines. A proper routine is necessary for success. So, what is your routine presently? It is much better to do a task for 5 mins everyday instead of only doing it once for 5 hours. The basic reason is that the mind learns better with consistency, and consistency is a key ingredient to being productive, which accounts for the success of many.

To break a task down into small steps and do it little by little every day consistently requires more strength than many can understand. When I wrote this book, I set aside 30mins per day to get it done, but I can tell you that there were days that seemed impossible to keep. The key is to do it until it becomes a habit and start small at first. You are not productive because you overload yourself with different tasks to do in a long duration of time; you become productive when your activity measures up to produce something. Routines help you develop a habit, which is something, but then also is the goal of aiming towards being successful.

These routines will eventually train you and discipline you into a force that must reach your dreams. Proper time management and being consistent with your work will create your luck. Luck is being prepared when the opportunity you desire presents itself, and you will be best able to take advantage of it when you prepare for it. Luck, for many people, is what they wait for to happen.

Roadmap

Having a roadmap is extremely handy when taking a journey with an impossible mission. You don't really need to have every step figured out, but just having a general idea of where you want to go is the most important thing. Try to find others that have also done something like what you want to do and if there is no one, then try to find something that resonates with you.

I basically knew what I wanted to do with Longyearbyen by making it more sustainable with locally produced greens, but I did not know how it would unfold.

At the time that I said it, I had no experience with growing food so far north and I could not find many others that were heading in that direction in town. Few people grew plants and vegetables in their homes, but that was more of a hobby. I was considering doing a larger scale commercial project and it would require many more resources than I could ever have expected.

Create Good Habits

The creation of good habits directly results from being disciplined and consistent. Good habits will put you in a better position for success in all areas of your life. I would suggest you decide, get passionate about it, and work on it consistently every day. Even if that is only 5 minutes, then give 120% of your energy for those 5 minutes to see your dreams come true. It takes time. Allowing our 'mood' to decide our behavior over our routines is one of the biggest mistakes I have made during my journey.

The key is to push through and get our goals done regardless of our 'mood' and develop the consistency that is needed to get there. A great way to keep these good habits you have developed is to write every day first thing in the morning. Take 10 minutes and write everything you desire in life with no restrictions. Think of it as a daily brainstorming session in your life. After you have done this, take the paper and keep it with you throughout the day. Refer to it during the day and visualize in your mind everything that you wrote there until you believe it.

When you do anything, refer to your list and see if that action is helping or hurting you to reach what you have written on your list. Those actions that are helping continue doing but stop doing things that contradict your list. Writing your desires daily is the fastest way to reach them!

Guidance

I have always tried to keep an open mind during the journey and can now say that many great ideas and some of the best suggestions came from people I did not know and have never met. Random people from all over the world would send me ideas, information, feedback, and love to help me reach my goals. I do not know how else to explain that, and I also do not understand why these people would invest time and energy into something that was not their own. Regardless of how I understood it, the fact remains that I could not have done what I did without guidance and support from many fans all over the world pushing me forward to complete the project. There were so many times when I wanted to quit, but I never did because the fans would not let me. When I would get frustrated and run out of ideas and patience, people would send me messages of support and ideas which would give me the energy I needed at the moment.

When I received the dome from James in Alaska, it was shipped in a large crate. He had built it in Alaska, took it apart, and then packaged it for us to rebuild on Svalbard. I did not know what to do with this enormous structure when I opened it, but sure enough, the people would come when the time was right. It was almost like the structure was building itself and the right person would come when we reached the level that required their skills. I have so many people to thank for helping me get things done there, and I appreciate you all. Nothing happens overnight and things take time to accomplish, so keep moving forward until you have exactly what you want.

Success may be difficult to reach, but it is not impossible, so stay persistent, committed, and you are halfway there. Consistency leads to developing good habits. Good habits lead to actions, and that leads to things getting done. This process will allow you to deal with the struggles and allow you to be patient enough to deal with the difficulties. Soon you realize that failure is a process and that once you learn the lesson from it, you can continue your journey and reach your goals.

CHAPTER

4

THE IMPOSSIBLE IS
POSSIBLE

It only seems impossible until it's done. -
Nelson Mandela

Do you believe the impossible is possible? Achieving the impossible starts with passion for what you are
doing and believing in yourself. You may not have it all
figured out just yet, but the path will open for you after
you make your decision and take the first step. From
someone who has attempted the impossible, the first
step will be to control the narrative. Impossible is just
a narrative, but it is not yours, because if you believe
the task to be impossible, you will not be attempting it.
Hence, you need to create a narrative that puts you in

charge. You have picked up a task which is daunting, hence your approach to it cannot be normal. The impossible does not become possible without acting from a powerful sense of imagination. A rational sense of visualizing the possibility of an impossible is vital to making it happen. Imagination steers up a lot of positive emotions and energy, which brings you to an emotional state of readiness to take up the task. If you are having an issue visualizing, you need to network with people who do not have a problem doing it. When you are with such people, they can gear you toward the path of visualizing your own goals of doing the impossible as well. It is a safe space for you to dream and say it out without being held back.

Think Positive and Act on it

Optimism is necessary for success in life, and possible for everyone to reach. Once you train yourself to be optimistic, it will have a positive effect on all your decisions and actions. The first step to achieving success is having a positive outlook on things. It is extremely difficult to do something in life if you keep telling yourself that it is not possible for you to do it. When you feel pessimism brewing up inside of you, ask yourself this question: Is this thought or emotion helping me or hurting me? Compare this thought to the list of desires you have written in the morning and evaluate it. Does it help you reach something on your list or is it keeping you from reaching something on your list? The more you practice this, then the easier it will be for you to stay positive and reach your goals.

As an optimist, one flaw to avoid while cultivating a nature of seeing the positive in everything is the desire to want to make everyone around you happy. Fact flash, everyone cannot be happy, and neither is it your responsibility to make that your mission. With people you cannot tell how what you do affects them, you can be kind to someone all the while and the person will stab you in the back, if not in the front. The goal you seek should be your focus, do what you can for people and expect less or nothing in return. Act out every positive thought you have, towards people and towards things and accept the response or consequence of such as constructive feedback but still maintain a positive mind in all.

Integrity

Getting loyal fans at the beginning of any project is extremely hard and costly. It is possible to take shortcuts, but that will not benefit you in the long run, and I would not recommend it. The most important thing to remember is to be true to yourself and who you are.

Whatever you do will eventually attract fans if you are dedicated enough, but do you want people around you for the wrong reasons? My mission was simple, to grow food near the North Pole and make Longyearbyen more sustainable, and then I stuck with it until I got momentum. The fans that followed me for this knew exactly what I wanted and what I was doing.

It was impossible, but I made it possible with thick skin and determination. I was honest with myself, and I could be honest with people who followed the journey. Just be yourself and everything will work out for the best! There is a selfish desire that comes with pursuing your goal. It can grow into something negative, which is away from making you a person of integrity. This is because integrity allows you to consider the collective good and not do things you know will directly cause the discomfort of another person. People with no integrity may not mind trampling on the collective good of the community, but a person of integrity or striving to be will not. Such persons should seek the collective good while finding how to balance this with their personal pursuit. Remember, once there is a will, it can automatically create a way. It may take a while for you to identify that way, but it is surely there, and you will surely find it if you keep at it.

Affirmations are key

Affirmations are key, and the things we say to ourselves hit deep into our realities. Affirmations tap directly into our consciousness (and even more with our unconsciousness) to motivate, push and challenge us towards reaching our full potential in life. No matter how you think or act on being positive, there are usually moments where those negative thoughts just stroll in through our defenses. Not to worry, you do not have a problem, you must counter those thoughts with affirmations. They are short powerful words and what they do best is erase your mind of all doubt on a subject. Ever seen someone lie so much about a particular thing? It sounds like the truth. These words can too, if you say them long enough, you will surely form a truth around them. The key is to keep saying it and set your mind open to believing it.

Many people are afraid of success and usually sabotage themselves when they are achieving the impossible. I have struggled with this fear many times before, and it usually results in resentment of those that are doing whatever you want to do. I began making excuses and stopping short of reaching my goals. It is important to deal with issues around fear of success as early as possible if you are to stand any chance of reaching the impossible. The best way to deal with this is to write affirmations and read them daily until you believe them. One that I love to write is: I deserve to be prosperous and wealthy.

It is impossible to write that and not have feelings

about it. Try it now and say it to yourself. "I deserve to be prosperous and wealthy".

How did it make you feel? What was the first thing that came to your mind?

We rarely know where the self-limiting beliefs are coming from, so I would recommend writing from different perspectives:

First person:

I deserve to be prosperous and wealthy.

Second person:

Ben, you deserve to be prosperous and wealthy.

Third person:

Ben deserves to be prosperous and wealthy.

This will allow you to deal with all angles and see where you resonate with each perspective. When you write, just make a note of the first thought that pops into your head. Once you get the hang of this, it will not take much time, but I recommend you do it daily. This will help to deal with the fear of success and get you moving forwards to your goal.

Growing Thick Skin

I started out as quite a shy and innocent guy growing up in Cleveland, OH in the US. That all changed by the time I moved to Svalbard and the place had so much potential. This started from my dream to make Svalbard green because it is such a unique place. I remember the first time I visited the archipelago, and I could not understand at all why people lived there. We went in the summer and all I could see were rocks everywhere. There are no large trees anywhere and it is a nightmare to measure distance in that place without visual cues. Everything looks so near, but if you decide to walk somewhere in the distance, you will walk for much longer than you realize. I also love how clear the air is there and how quiet it is. There is a silence there that I have not experienced in other parts of the world except maybe in Antarctica. My dream to travel the world was happening more than I realized it would, and soon I took it for granted how often I was traveling. Svalbard was a place for me to make my American dream come true. I never felt at home in the States and for the first time that I can remember, I felt like I have arrived. When deciding between doing my project on Svalbard and returning home to Florida, it was already decided. I would do this project on Svalbard no matter what.

Deciding like that sure had other factors that would convince me otherwise, however, as I continued the path, I developed thick skin to such influences. It is funny how the world heeds to your desire once you really make it the core of your existence. As humans, one of our powers is the ability to adapt to the situations and circumstances we face. This can be a bad thing when all you want to do is adapt and not become better. In another situation, this can be a lifesaving skill. For example, when life deals you a card you were not prepared for, you can either complain about it or change the narrative. In this situation, we usually just deal with it and limit our ability to reach higher. In your adaptation process, developing a thick skin is vital in order to deal with the criticism that is sure to come when you reach for your dreams.

THE BUCK STOPS HERE

Accept responsibility for your life. Know that it is you who will get you where you want to go, no one else. - Les Brown

There comes a time in life when you finally understand that you must be responsible for everything you do. It can be scary, but it can also be rewarding depending on your perspective. To be responsible can be very confusing for many because being responsible means not only you took part in the occurrence of an event actively but also that your inaction may have been your participation. Either side can be measured as good or bad, and it all depends on the perspective at play. Of course, it should not be difficult to acknowledge being responsible when the product is positive, but what happens when it is not? This is where the major task is. When things go wrong, would you still be confident enough to take responsibility?

Take Responsibility

The moment you stop blaming others for your situation is the moment that you truly become free! You are exactly where you are now, based on the choices that you made to get you here. Many of those choices are not consciously made, so it can be confusing when we see the results of such choices. The buck stops with you, and it is now time that you accept this responsibility. If you understand the truth about taking responsibility for your actions, do so more often regardless of the negative consequences you will have to deal with. Taking responsibility builds confidence in you as a person, and confidence is always a positive thing to have. Confidence is a trait that is embedded in the personality of successful people. If you want to be successful at anything in life, you need to be confident. Taking responsibility would build this in you.

To take that first step towards being responsible and taking responsibility, exercise your power of choice. Yes, we all have a choice and to say you do not means you are shying away from being responsible. When something unfortunate happens to us that is beyond our control, we still can choose how we respond to the situation. As responsible as you are for your choices, so are you for the consequences that follow. The brighter side to it all is that you get to gain more experience in making better choices, to being optimistic and even to being free. Freedom requires that you take responsibility and oversee your life, not blaming others for how you have turned out or how far you achieve your goal. It may have been tough for you, but there was always a choice for your during the process.

Improve and get better

It was a process to get where I am today, and there were so many mistakes made that created opportunities for me to improve and get better. No one gets it all right the first time and the mistakes are where all the magic happens. As soon as you think you are good enough, or know enough, then all learning stops, and things stagnate. The most valuable lesson I have learned so far is that there is something to be learned from everyone. Passionate people cannot help but share their passion with you, so what is this person passionate about? This is also where listening comes into play, and why it is so important to listen carefully. In Permaculture, feedback is critical to making the design better and for improving. Without feedback, mistakes would continue to be made and flaws would never be corrected. As I was designing Polar Permaculture, and making Svalbard green, I would notice things that did not add up. Why do we import everything there only to ship it all back to the mainland as waste after?

Why do we import all food, but then dump it into the sea as organic waste after? My thoughts moved from this linear resource line to thinking more circularly. How could I make Longyearbyen more of a circular economy and extract more from the resources we imported there? This is where I got the idea to do a zero-waste restaurant, which would not only focus on producing food but also on dealing with the waste that was created during the process. Being able to grow local food, and then composting the organic material into fertilizer that could grow more food, just made sense to me. Why dump it all into the sea and release all that energy for free? It is super expensive to ship items up to Svalbard, and to ship it back 1500 km (932 miles) to the mainland. Polar Permaculture was concerned, and sought to change, by breaking this linear model and creating a circular economy around food production.

Listen Carefully

Listening has been a skill that has taken me the

longest to learn and eventually master. I have always heard people but have not been patient enough to listen. I have found that by actively listening to anyone, you can learn so much more than you ever imagined. There is an opportunity to learn from anyone in any situation. My daughter Vlasa is such a wise young lady, and I have learned so much more from her than I feel I have taught her. I have a terrible habit of finishing people's sentences for them, and I do not understand why I do that. I might think I know what they are going to say, but it is more important that I let them say it and I listen carefully to what they have said. Listening carefully has opened many doors for me and has created unique opportunities beyond what I could have imagined. The more we help others get what they want, the easier it is for us to get what we want. Listen first to what others have to say before you ask your questions. Respect their time and value it to see more opportunities presented to you as a direct result.

Accountability

Accountability and honesty run together parallel with each other. It is important to be honest about your results and the outcome of your efforts. By accepting and learning from your mistakes, you will move a step closer to success. When you make a mistake, then admit it and learn from it. Try not to do it again and come back ready to try again tomorrow. Who do you answer to regarding the journey you have to achieve the impossible? What happens if you do not do what you say, and things do not move quickly like you have expected? The plan will take longer and there is also the option that it will not happen at all. The situation can get much more complicated when there is no accountability, so I would suggest having someone to answer to and who can advise you like a mentor.

Learn From Others

I wish I would have taken more time to learn from others before making all the mistakes myself. Many have had similar challenges and issues to what I was dealing with during the running of Polar Permaculture, but I wanted to do everything myself. If I had to do it over again, I would have taken more time to plan and see what others have done in similar situations to reduce the learning curve I had experienced. I could also work with so many interesting people from around the world and have been able to learn much from them. Many of them had great experience and knowledge, but I was often too busy trying to make money to take advantage of it. Polar Permaculture was started as a food production company, but quickly became a tourism company to pay bills. It might have been smarter to make it a non-profit company, but then I would have had to focus on fund-raising instead of focusing on profit. I am not so sure that it is easier to raise money for a non-profit than it is to find money selling products as a for profit company. What I am sure of is that others have faced these similar challenges, and it would have been wise to reach out to those folks and get advice beforehand.

Develop and Use Your Tools

Creating a circular economy on Svalbard took many more resources than I had imagined and required skills that went well beyond my skill set alone. I needed to find equipment that I have never used before, and this was further complicated by the logistics of having to order everything online. I could not just visit a local supplier and touch the equipment. I could only read descriptions online and ask many questions via email, which also became challenging. Research is a primary industry on Svalbard, and you would think that it would be possible to work with someone there regarding this, but most of the research is Arctic based, and not concerned about food production, unfortunately. I never understood why no one else on Svalbard was asking these questions or concerned about our food supply. Perhaps everyone just took it for granted that the supply ships would continue to come like they always have, but many other cultures around the Arctic are growing their own food, so why not on Svalbard? The most important skill that I have developed during this project would be working with other people. Sharpen your tools and keep your toolbox up to standard. You never know when that tool that you have will be required, so having it ready will put you two steps ahead of the others.

CHAPTER

6

BE PRESENT

You don't build a bond without being present.
- James Earl Jones

Being present means being fully aware of exactly what is happening around you. Seize the day and gain all the experience from what is being presented to you right now. All you have is right now, so do not put off your goals because of being busy or lack of money. The right time never actually comes, and you just need to make the most of this moment. Living in the now, and not just 'living' it, but also giving it the passion and respect that it deserves. Focus all your energy on this moment and this moment alone. To live in the moment speaks to being evidently conscious with all your senses majoring on being aware and present. A promise of a better day is still a promise, but the future is better because people are presently working towards it. If you intend to see any result in the future that matches your desire, get to work now. Life is more meaningful and valuable when captured in the present. It is normal to have expectations, aspirations, and vision for the future, but your focus should be on the little things you can do now to make such happen. Train your mind to focus on the current task or activity. Engage the present as though it is your last, with all vigor and consciousness, and then you can savor all the beauty in such moments.

Be Bold

Being bold does not need to be a bad thing! Being bold to me means standing up for what you believe. Being bold is really an admirable trait that many people desire and makes those who have it appear stronger at will. Bold people see fear for what it really is, an illusion. They hold their head high and go through a situation with a sense of purpose and stability. To be bold is not to excuse the possibility of risk when attempting a task, it is to let the benefits outweigh the risk, which allows you to move on to grab life by the horns and deliver on the task. To be bold, you will have to do away with fears that hold you back. This does not just happen instantly. It takes time, but you must act on it. Look at something you have always been scared to do and set out to it. Give yourself a timeline to complete the task. Little by little, you are training the mind to let go of the need to hold onto those fears. The magic happens when you see that you automatically become bold to do a task you will have otherwise not attempted.

So many people laughed at me and called me crazy when I did this project. They all thought it would fail and that it would not last long at all. They were all wrong and truly did not understand what Svalbard needed quite like I did; I suppose. Polar Permaculture was started in 2015 officially, but I have been working on this project on Svalbard since 2012. If I would have listened to the first person who made fun of me, then I would not have carried this on for so long, and I had to develop a thick skin to get through. I highly recommend you do the same if you are planning to do the impossible because the amount of people that will laugh at you and tell you it can never be done will be huge. It is one thing to listen to constructive criticism and decide to pivot your course for best results, but another thing entirely to listen and quit on your dream. Be bold and fulfill your destiny! You can do this.

M e d it at e

Mediation is a powerful tool for stress relief and being present in the moment. There are many types to choose from, so do not feel pressured to do what your best friend has suggested to you. By meditating and finding inner peace, you can be more present and in the now. It is also a great way to relax and to get rid of negative thoughts. Depending on the type of mediation you prefer, wear something comfortable and stay hydrated. Find the best time of day to meditate and work it into your routine. Another key to meditation is working with your breath and learning how to do it correctly. I prefer dance meditations and struggle to sit still long enough to enter a deep state. I suppose it also depends on the time of day that I would meditate, because I also enjoy sitting quietly and emptying my mind. The main thing is that you do meditation that works for you.

Gratitude is Important

Gratitude and living in the moment go well together! It is difficult to not be grateful for the little important things without being present because you would surely miss them. Gratitude is not so much about being grateful for the big wins or the small wins. It is about appreciating life in all its goodness. There are truly good things in this life, but only those who are grateful will receive more of it. Gratitude is one of the most overlooked tools to unlock the beauties of this world. The sense of entitlement masking the world would not allow many people to see this. So many people think they deserve all the opportunities that come their way. Hard work and being grateful should not be exclusive to each other.

While you put yourself into your goal or a particular task and it turns out great as you desired, you ought to be thankful. If you truly think of it, you will discover hard work alone is not enough. Being grateful opens you up to achieve more and become more. It also improves your physical and psychological health greatly as people who are grateful are proven to be happier. You even see yourself deal with a lot of insecurities as you become more grateful. Your self-esteem would improve as you show gratitude to people.

Encouragement

It is easy to think about ourselves and what we have accomplished, but no one is an island. We can not do anything by ourselves and no matter how much we think it is about us, it really is not. Work to build up fans and encourage them to be successful, and this will only create more success for yourself. I feel the more you give that the more you receive, and I work to see things from as many perspectives as possible. Encourage your fans to be the best they can be and encourage them to follow their own dreams as well. Use my example as a way for you to follow and build your own dreams. What are you waiting for?

CHAPTER

7

TAKE A CHANCE

Great success is built on failure,
frustration, even catastrophe. -
Sumner Redstone

The key is to step out of your comfort zone and not be afraid to try new things. What is stopping you from learning a new skill or growing your own food, for example? Push yourself to get new experiences and, therefore, bring more excitement into your life. A comfort zone is when you are in that mental state that equates to being most content and this could be in relation to anything: life, work, your goals, and so on. It is indeed a good place to be, however, to settle in such a state hinders growth. Another benefit to stepping out of your comfort zone is that it builds self-confidence, which is a good thing even for your mental health. Being successful can be compared to jumping from a prominent place and pulling your parachute open to land safely. You would not start with the highest jump in the beginning, and it makes more sense to start small. Many bumps and set-backs will occur along the way, but the most important thing is to remember to jump. If you never jump, then for sure your parachute will not open, but how beautiful it is when you do, and it finally does? That is where the magic happens, and you will find joy.

Svalbard

Svalbard in Norwegian literally means "the cold edge" and it feels like it when you arrive there. After flying one and a half hours from Oslo, you then arrive in Tromsø which is considered "Paris of the north" and is an amazing city. From Tromsø, you need to fly another one and a half hours north in order to reach the Svalbard archipelago. The islands were discovered by the Dutch and used extensively for whale hunting during the 17th and 18th centuries. The largest island is Spitsbergen, and it is what the Treaty of 1920 was named after to agree between the nations. Norway was granted sovereignty of the islands when the treaty took effect on 14 August 1925. This meant that Svalbard would be governed by Norway, but they must respect the other countries' right to commerce on the islands. The following countries had an interest in Svalbard: Denmark, France, Italy, Japan, the Netherlands, Norway, Sweden, the United Kingdom, and the United States. There are no visas required to enter, but you may require a visa to enter Norway. There are few options for direct access to Svalbard without first going through Norway, and the most common way of arrival is via flight.

Longyearbyen

Longyearbyen is the capital of Svalbard and where the largest percentage of the population lives. This is the "northernmost" city in the world and lies 78 degrees north. With a population of around 2100 people in the village, the local council has responsibility for regulating activities where people live and for the infrastructure. There is more infrastructure available on the island, and I think most people take it for granted. Being so isolated from the mainland, it is important to offer the residents activities to keep them busy and to deal with the extremes in the seasons that occur in the town. Longyearbyen is known as quite a tourist destination, and it is possible to see things there that are not available in other locations.

CO2 Output

If Svalbard was an independent country, it would have one of the highest CO_2 outputs per capita. The island is powered by one of the few coal power plants in Norway and the supply lines are extremely long. A strange fact that I learned while being there is that all organic waste and sewage is dumped directly into the sea with no treatment. This means that whatever you put in the toilet will end up in the sea. Being a place with plenty of fish, you would expect to eat fresh fish most of the time, but it is not possible in town. The fish is for private use only, which means you can catch it during the short season and eat it yourself but may not sell or buy it for commercial use. The plan has been for many years now to set up a local fishing industry, but at the time of this writing, it has not happened yet. There are also some reindeer, but not enough to have a local meat industry, and most of the reindeer is imported from Scandinavia. It is such a luxury to go to Svalbard, and I always laugh when journalists say they are going to Svalbard to do a story on climate change. Just going to Svalbard contributes so much CO2 that I am not even sure if it is the best option.

Zero-Waste

Longyearbyen operates on an extreme linear supply line and the vision for Polar Permaculture was to reduce this. The plan was to make a zero-waste restaurant on the island, and this would have been a revolutionary concept for the place. All restaurants on Svalbard totally depend on raw materials from the mainland, and all waste from the island is shipped back to the mainland for processing. Whatever organic waste that is produced is dumped into the sea, and then more inputs are shipped up from the mainland. We dump plenty of energy and resources into the sea only to ship it all back up again at a premium. Why not reuse these resources if possible and get multiple uses out of them? What if instead of dumping that food waste into the sea, we could compost it and use the fertilizer created from it to grow more food locally? Instead of shipping spent cooking oil back 1500 km (932 miles) to Tromsø to be recycled, what if we can make biogas from it and use it to power growing lights for example? These are all the questions I asked myself in my quest to set up a zero-waste restaurant.

Circular Economy

Is it possible to create a circular economy in such a remote and challenging location? What does a circular economy mean? Why is it important in such a remote location as Svalbard? My thinking with Polar Permaculture was to create a circular economy around food production and move away from the linear model which is presently being used. I had to think about the complete system and break it down into manageable steps to make it make sense. The important thing was to grow crops that have a high profit margin and that also sprout. Microgreens are quite popular with chefs regarding being used as garnish, salads, and for sandwiches.

There is also research that shows Microgreens are healthy and they taste delicious. Polar Permaculture would grow these Microgreens in trays of 18 to 20 pots and sell a tray for about 450,- nok or (US$45) which would generate a decent profit. Normally, the waste that is generated from such greens that are imported from Europe is thrown into the garbage bin and the energy lost. We delivered fresh greens to the restaurants and would offer the option to compost the waste that was left over from the greens we delivered. That is the first example of a company on the island taking responsibility for the waste created from their products, and we would compost this organic waste and reuse the plastic containers.

The compost that was created would be given away to folks interested in using it to feed their plants and for home use. This created a circle regarding food production. Our efforts inspired the city to become green, and they also started an initiative to create a circular economy in Longyearbyen based on: Food production, energy production, and waste management. Who would have known that our humble project would also move Longyearbyen forwards from a linear to a more circular economy? This was a long process, and I could not change everything overnight. It is a process where I just take the small steps necessary and continue to try new things. Does it not get boring doing the same things repeatedly? My biggest fear is that by not trying new things and continuing to learn each day, I would have regrets and I promised myself that I will regret nothing in life.

Be Open-minded and Value the Journey

Being open-minded and open to adventures will make life more exciting and fun. Being open-minded means accepting that we do not know everything, and that there are things we could be wrong about. That means we should be ready to change our ideas, opinions, and thoughts as we learn from our experiences. Every stage in life has its own benefits, and it is wise to make the best of such as life is short. Do not be an overachiever, running into the future and forgetting to live out the present. Life is a journey which does not happen all at once, but some days are good, others are not so good. Enjoy it anyway. The journey of life is also personal. Although you get to have similar experiences with other people, you still control your reaction to life ultimately. To embrace the journey of life and live in the moment, show gratitude and more. Expressing your gratitude is not in recognizing when there is a major win, but also in setbacks. Be grateful for the lessons learned, and it is a healthier way to live. Stay committed to your goals.

Those who live life purposefully have a better chance at valuing the journey. They understand the concept of the process and walk through the thick and thin towards their goal. Also, there is a need to take your network seriously. Having a purpose in life might not require the input of others externally, but life is better lived when you can connect with a few other like minded people. That when the time requires that you fall back on your support system, you have one to fall on. It can be depressing when you walk through the journey of life alone. Getting by major obstacles in life would require the input of others. I always grin at having too many tasks on one's plate, because it is not the best way to do life. It may be good to know how to multitask and sometimes, it can be a big life saver, but to make all your life about multitasking is such a horrible way to live in my opinion. Learning is also crucial to valuing the journey of life. As mentioned earlier, life does not happen all at once, so also is learning. You cannot learn it all at once, hence pace yourself in learning as you go through life. Lessons learned can be a powerful motivator to enjoying life, especially on the hard, and there are hard days.

Seeds

There are a few different edible plants on Svalbard, and one of the most popular seed vaults in the world. The Global seed vault is home to many seeds. Seeds were the most important resource that we had and are what made everything possible. I have never been in the Global seed vault and missed the one opportunity that presented itself for me to visit. I regret it, but there is not much to do about it now, and there is plenty of information available about it online. They have seeds stored there from all over the world, and I reached out to them to get some seeds to work with them. They mentioned they were aware of my project and that they supported our work but could not offer any seeds. It makes sense when you think about it because they are just like a bank holding seeds for those organizations and countries that have deposited them there.

My understanding is that the only time seeds have been taken out was when they were sent to Syria via Lebanon to replace a crop that was devastated by war. The story goes that these crops were grown and more seeds harvested. Some of these seeds were then returned back to the seed vault, and the mission was accomplished. It is one of the most popular destinations on Svalbard and I never understood why until I heard this story. I used to feel bad taking tourists there because you cannot enter and can only look at the building from outside. At the time of writing, there is no information about anything, and it gives off a cold and unwelcoming feeling. A seed can be in the form of many things, so choose your seeds carefully and give them plenty of love when you plant them. This goes for actual seeds, thoughts, ideas, people, love, and anything else that applies.

Super Fans

I have had a few super fans during the time building up Polar Permaculture, and they make everything worth it. There have been many difficulties growing food near the North Pole, and one of my super fans, Thomas, always had a way of cheering me up when I was down. He would come to visit once a year because of his love for Svalbard. I think Svalbard attracts a special type of person and if I had to narrow it down to one person, then it would be Thomas. He came to Svalbard because he loved the place and has been coming there for many years. When he found out about my project, he made time and energy to help us succeed. Thomas is from Denmark and would send us many types of seeds and he also became a family friend. I do not think I could have done all of this without support from Thomas and am grateful that I have him in my life even until today. We still speak to each other and check in with each other, but we both are not doing well because of the situation on Svalbard and with the world.

Don't be afraid to try

This does not mean that you put yourself in harm or risk your health and safety in search of an adventure. It also does not mean putting yourself or others' lives in danger for your cause. What I mean is that it is important to let yourself out of the shell that makes you feel safe and at ease. Fact is, it is not trying that people are afraid of; it is failing. If you were guaranteed one hundred percent that you would succeed at a particular thing, you might be more motivated. Although we do not have such guarantees that are absolute, we do however have to try something new to avoid being stuck at a certain place for too long a time. Being opened to trying something new does not include the things that are obviously harmful to our health or our goals. One of the major reasons you should not be afraid of trying new things is that you do not want to live with regrets of not trying. Regrets limit our advancement as they increasingly keep us in the past, wallowing in the guilt of not getting something done or not making a certain decision.

You never know what you might find when you try, but it is safe to say there is a big possibility of finding something great, just as there is a possibility of finding otherwise. The good part, however, is that you would have tried, which builds in your self-confidence in approaching other possibly unrelated issues of life. That boldness that comes with knowing you tried is second to none. Remember, you can never really achieve your goals if you focus and dwell on the fears that are in your way. No one accomplishes anything by allowing their fears to conquer them. Take it like this: you only live once and to not try is to think there is another better time to be more prepared to try. If you try it and fail, it makes you even more interesting. Failures do not define people who see beyond their failures. See beyond and get on with life learning and doing the impossible regardless of the fear.

Failure

Fear of failure is obvious, because who wants to fail and be embarrassed? No one I know would want to fail, but fear of failure prevents many from trying at all or ever getting anything done. Mistakes are learning experiences and once you realize, it is easier to make calculated moves and reach your goals. I have not been so consumed with fear of failure and, in fact, have embraced my mistakes and continued to work towards my goal. I think it is important to develop thick skin, so that it is much easier to deal with different opinions and when things do not go your way.

If you never try, then for sure you will not accomplish your impossible mission, but if you try, then the odds become more 50/50. You will never know unless you try, so my suggestion is that you make the most of it and give it all you have. Success demands overcoming obstacles and maybe even failing sometimes. The most important thing to remember is to get up, dust yourself off, and try again. Clinging to what is 'easy' and avoiding doing what is needed to be done will severely limit your chances of success. You have a goal set; you cannot be redundant about it. Take charge and learn to overcome the obstacles in your path.

WORDS ARE THINGS

I am convinced that words are things, and we simply don't have the machinery to measure what they are. I believe that words are tangible things. - Maya Angelou

Words and language are unique to human beings only and have extreme power to be used for bad and good. Most people do not realize how powerful words are and how much they change the world around them. Regardless of whether it is used to express love, instructions for building something, or as the rally cry before a major battle, the words we use can create the future. If you think about it, the words we use probably linger longer in our memories than actual faces or events.

Words are things and have amazing power which needs to be dealt with carefully. Whether they are spoken or written, words are truly powerful, and they shape our world in ways we cannot see. Our preferred choice of words sets the parameters by which we live, but it can be complicated. Although, the true power of words is in what they mean, how they are conveyed, and how they are being interpreted.

Determining the meaning of events in our lives, and our responsibility to choose to find an empowering meaning, are some of the most important things we can ever grasp. If we choose a disempowering meaning that is our choice. When something happens to us, we can consciously control our verdict on the positive or negative meaning behind it. Our first reactions to something are not always conscious, but then we can step in and reframe the meaning. For example, let us say you failed a test. Does this mean that you are a failure? Or does this mean that you now know areas you need to work on improving? That is up to us to determine, and even if we feel like a failure initially, we can step in and transform what the failure means to us internally. We can cultivate a positive interpretation of nearly all events in our lives. Some call it looking for the silver lining or relentless optimism.

How does this have anything to do with the power of words you may wonder? Words can often have one meaning, just like failing a test. However, words do not have the dynamic range and malleability that our interpretation of life does. The definition of a cat differs from the definition of a dog, and no rose-colored glasses can change that. So, we have more leeway to determine an empowering meaning from events than we do from words. Ugly means ugly, ugly does not mean pretty. The power of words comes into play when we define our reality.

The words we use in our minds repeatedly to describe ourselves and our identity are some of the most powerful forces in our lives. If we constantly utter self deprecating language in our internal dialogue, we are allowing the power of words to work against us. Telling ourselves that we are fat, weak, worthless, or stupid can sap us of our power to find the positive meaning from our experiences. If we tell ourselves we are stupid all day, then when we fail a test, we can seldom see the perspective that it may have a silver lining. We are much more likely to use it to affirm our belief that we are stupid. "See, I failed. I am stupid." When we speak, write, think, or otherwise use words, we are engaging in something we should be mindful of. The power of words in our world is undeniable. Our linguistic ability can set us on a trajectory to achieve great things or to remain disenchanted with our lives.

Words inspire Belief

Can you remember someone saying something that made you feel insecure? Things like "You have an enormous nose", "you smell", "you need to smile more", causing you to become insecure with yourself. As a result, you subconsciously learn to cover your nose so it can not be seen, or you get nervous when people come close to you. The reason this happens will eventually become buried in your mind, but the damage done cannot be reversed unless you address it. The same goes the other way when we receive compliments. The power of telling someone they are a great artist vs. telling them they are terrible is real, and it has been documented. Fear of speaking is real and comes from a lack of confidence.

When we have something to say, but are too shy to say it, then we keep quiet. The best way to overcome this fear is to speak until it feels comfortable. If you are not a brilliant speaker, then you must fool yourself until you believe you are a skilled speaker. The more you speak, then the better you will become, so just get out there and say what you need to say. Learn from the mistakes and develop a thick skin to deal with the criticism. You can do this, and you are indeed an impressive speaker.

Leading

Leading is an important skill that will be necessary to complete your mission. Unless you can do everything yourself, you will eventually need to manage a team that can work to reach your dream. I would not recommend doing everything yourself, even if you can do it all because you are limited by time. It will be best to focus your time on the task that you do best. Let others support you and find the best people within your budget. I did not want to be a leader, but then I soon realized that nothing would happen unless I did. Leading is the way to move your team closer to reaching your impossible mission. You can do this, and I am sure you will be fine! Having a team that shares a common goal with you can make all the difference in achieving the impossible. Leadership then gives the passion and energy a focus and direction.

As a leader, it is your responsibility to make everyone in your team welcome. They are not just there because of you; they are there because they believe in the dream you believe in and consider themselves valuable to bringing it to reality. No matter how small a team member contributes, you ought to make them feel valuable. The responsibility for you starts with identifying people who are genuine enough to be part of your team, then comes the place of managing every one of them individually and collectively. Leadership is not only in holding a title; it is being responsible for the productive output of your team members.

Coaching

After you learn something, it is important to teach it to someone else in order to master the skill. It is scary to coach and teach others because we can sometimes doubt our skills and abilities. Being a coach does not mean you need to be perfect, and I find it is more of a two-way street than is to be expected. Coaching can be a fun way to sharpen your skills and see other's perspective on the task at hand. When we do things, it is easy to assume that our way is the only way, but what if you work with someone and they have a smarter, quicker way to achieve the same results? How would you know unless you give them a chance to show you what they can do?

Coaching can bridge the gap, and this can only happen when you are not afraid of sharing and receiving feedback. Many people feel the more knowledge they keep to themselves, the more relevant they are. They base their definition of relevance on having information others do not have or have access to. However, being relevant in this fast paced world goes way beyond that. If knowledge of a certain information is the only thing that makes you relevant, there will come a time another person will have such information and just like that, your relevance is deflated. Coaching makes you more valuable and relevant, as the person being coached would have been affected for life. If you think of your learning process very well, can you boastfully say all you know now was pre-programmed into your head? Definitely not. You also gained it from somewhere, built on it and now you ought to pass it on to others.

Develop your Vocabulary

The words we use can drive us forward to success or contribute to our own downfall. There are people (Speakers) who make their money just from the words they choose, and it is what separates the good ones from the bad ones. They use their vocabulary to tell a story with their voices and engage the audience as well as generate their paychecks. We have all had unique experiences with our teachers, both past and present, and I am sure that you still carry emotional baggage related to some of these experiences. Many of our teachers meant well, but they did not know our true capabilities or where we would end up after school. There is much more emotion to the relationship that does not meet the eye. Teachers can make judgment calls and say things that have so much influence on our thoughts and actions.

Have you ever had a teacher say you would not be successful, or that you are always causing trouble? Teachers mean well, but they are not the most successful people in the world now, are they? Many successful people have dropped out of school completely and still did their impossible mission and found the success they were looking for. If you do not understand the importance of words, you may find it difficult understanding the need for having a better form of expressing your words when people seem unclear about it. When you have a team you work closely with, you must work on your expressions. Learn how to use other expressions to help them understand how you feel, to boost their confidence and to give them encouragement.

Say you 'can' instead of you 'can't'

The difference between these two words has decided many events that have shaped history. As soon as you say you can not do something, all creativity to make it happen shuts down and it will never happen. When you say you can do something, perhaps you do not know how you will do it, but your mind comes up with solutions. A can-do trait is not just about the words you say, it is also your attitudinal display to a particular task. Your words must match your action to birth the positivity you hope to create. If you have a negative attitude, it will taint your entire outlook on life and dramatically decrease your ability to succeed. Instead of consciously crafting a successful life, your negative disposition will often lead to a passive personality, one in which you shrug your shoulders and let life happen to you, rather than making things happen for you.

If that is not the life you imagined for yourself, then it is time to transform your current attitude into a can-do attitude. It begins with your mindset, the way you think the critical factor between someone who achieves success vs. someone who does not comes down to your mindset. Our mindset determines the way we deal with tough situations and setbacks, as well as our willingness to deal with and improve ourselves. After you have heavily invested in your mindset, then match it up with a concurrent action. Most of my experiences working with Polar Permaculture were positive ones and heavily influenced by fans. I had people that I never met before contacting me for tours, meetings, and ideas. This showed me that what I was doing was not for nothing and that it was necessary. The negative experiences that I faced in the beginning were now changing to more positive experiences. When I first started this project, everyone laughed and called me crazy, but now people were calling me a genius and loving what I was doing with the place.

NEVER STOP LEARNING

He who learns but does not think, is lost.
He who thinks but does not learn is in great
danger. - Confucius

School is not the only place to learn, but many of us cannot realize that. Learning is a constant and ongoing process of evolution that first involves acknowledging you do not know everything. This is an important concept in shaping your personality, introducing new concepts and ideas to you, and removing any limitations. The worst thing you could do to yourself is to think you know everything. Choose to continue to learn, grow and develop every day. When you learn something, work to master it and then to teach it to others. This also means that you are humble enough to accept feedback and be open for improvement.

Learn and get better everyday

This is imperative if you are to become the best version of yourself! Understand that whatever you know now is current, but stay open to new information that adds value to what you already know. Be flexible in learning new knowledge and facts instead of refusing the truth based on your experiences. I would say again it is a two-way street regarding support for fans, and that for as many fans that have encouraged me to keep going, I have also encouraged them to deal with issues they were facing. It felt great to give and receive advice and to know that there was a network in place that was alive with information exchange. If people had issues with something that I could support with, then I would make the recommendation, and I had no issues with fans doing the same for me. There are many forms of support with financial being only one, and I believe that sometimes emotional support is more important than financial support.

Never stop learning

I can think of so many reasons it is important to never stop learning and can not think of one logical reason you should not. What about you? Do you have a logical reason it is not important to continue learning? It was important for me to share my experience and knowledge with others, and I worked to be as accessible as possible. I saw my fans as an extension of me and felt I could access their education and knowledge when needed to deal with issues that I faced. Fans range when dealing with Svalbard, and many people that followed me were interested in what was happening there. I also had others from around the Arctic reaching out to me, and we would share what we have learned with each other. This educational exchange helped us to build a stronger awareness of what was happening and helped us to make better decisions in our daily lives.

Become a lifelong learner

It is a process, and no one is perfect with this process, but the more you practice, the better you will become.

To become a lifelong learner, it is important to change your mindset and concepts. Make learning a priority and embrace the journey while learning from everyone. We can learn from anyone, and I have learned the most from the people I have least expected to learn from. No one knows everything, and when you think about it, we need to tap into the expertise of those around us. Many of the fans of Polar Permaculture were scientists, researchers, business people, and many more. Everyone had different ideas about what I was doing and how I could do it better. I kept an open mind and was always looking for feedback.

This is an important principle in Permaculture: apply self-regulation and feedback, which means looking at what you have done and working to make it better.

> "Live as if you were to die tomorrow.
> Learn as if you were to live forever."
> Mahatma Gandhi

Lifelong learning is a common trait among influential thinkers, leaders, and influencers. By being a lifelong learner, you will become more valuable and useful to those around you. Learn from life and understand that all learning does not come from school or in books. Are there others that you could work with that have similar objectives as you and are going in a parallel direction? This synergy created between such projects can also help to propel you toward your success and create a win/ win situation between all involved. I have learned that common goals usually connect people, and that there is no I in team. Use synergy as much as possible when you are working to accomplish your dreams and you will not regret it at all.

LEARN FROM FAILURE

LEARN FROM FAILURE. If you are an entrepreneur and your first venture wasn't a success, welcome to the club. - Richard Branson

In life, there will be difficulties, but the powerful individual is the one who pulls through just about everything. The way to win is to push through the failure and keep moving towards your goal.

Rejection is your friend

Rejection and failure are not the same for everyone and I wonder what the difference is. Some people take rejection and quit, while others take rejection and come back stronger. I think timing is everything and just because you were rejected now does not mean you will be rejected tomorrow.

How do we know when we are on the right path or if we have strayed away from our cause? Feedback is one of the most effective ways that I have used to correct courses and get back on track. Constructive criticism is much needed and having thick skin to deal with it is also a plus. No one does everything perfectly, and it is always important to develop into the best versions of ourselves that we can. I do not see mistakes as failures at all and have learned so much from the mistakes that I have made. There is a fine line, however, because some mistakes will put you out of business quickly. The important thing is to develop a sound foundation, and this is only possible when we accept feedback and use it to improve ourselves.

Perspective

Seeing things from a different perspective is what it takes to get a bird's-eye view of what you are working on.

Many times, the mind can play tricks on us, and things are not always as they appear to us. What are others doing that could benefit you, and how could you gain that knowledge? My suggestion would be to watch what they do and observe their habits. We are a collection of what we do and by observing others in action, we can get a better perspective on their true character. This also applies to us, and we should always observe our habits and who we spend our time with. This will allow us to get a perspective on our situation and allow us to continue moving forwards regardless of what others say.

Failures are leading the path to success

Many failures and mistakes actually led the path. This might be difficult to understand, but many of the biggest companies in the world started out small at one time. When you learn to read the signs and adjust course as needed, then you align yourself with success and what it means to you.

If you are not coachable, then it will not be possible for you to receive the guidance that is offered by others. Many times, on your way to success, you will go off course and this is perfectly normal. Who will guide you during those moments, and will you heed the calls given? Many times, the information comes from unlikely sources, so keeping an open mind will be a great way to fast track your success.

Listen and Learn

Keeping an open mind would be the most valuable idea that I have learned during my experience. I have been in many strange situations, and it is always so easy to judge others and jump to conclusions. Not everyone does things the way we do. This is a fact and something that we should learn and accept. There are at least 6 different ways to do anything, and to expect everyone to do it our way is selfish. When someone wants to do something for you, see how they do it first. Perhaps you will learn something new, and you can always give you feedback after. If they ask for your advice on how to do it, then that is great. Just coach them and send them on their way. Never think that you know everything! There is always something new to learn each day.

*It's a success if you
have learned something*

Failure is an amazing experience, and I have learned the most from many situations where I thought I failed. Failure allowed me to pivot, learn something new, adjust course, and move forward with my ambitions. Progress is more important than perfection and I am a huge fan of keeping things simple and getting it done before getting it good.

Experiencing a major failure is one of the worst things in life. It fills you with negative emotions and leaves you feeling worthless. Therefore, most people will do anything within their power to avoid failure, even if this means attempting nothing new. Despite the negative energy it comes with, failure has its positive side. Experiencing failure can teach you lessons that you would not have learned otherwise - you can learn from failure. Some of the most successful people in the world could only attain success because of the lessons they learned from their previous failures.

Aside from the valuable technical lesson that failure will teach you in relation to the goal you pursue, it will teach you that life does not guarantee success at all. Yes, we succeed, and we also fail, such is life. This lesson is not to dampen the fire of positivity in us, but to get us to keep trying. Sometimes, the factors responsible can be out of your control, so it is not even always about the measure of your input. Another major lesson to be learned from failing is the ability to embrace change. Change, as they say, is constant. If you failed at something, then it means you must have not done something in the right way. And even if you did all things in the right way, you may not have figured out what has gone wrong. If you are too rigid to the call, you may end up not learning from your mistake.

Failure is not final, it is just part of the process, and the more you learn to walk past your failures, the less likely you are to keep failing. The failures in the past will widen your horizon in knowledge and experience and this also affects your perspective. A broad perspective is a blessing to one seeking success at doing the impossible. It means you can reason a task at a much wider angle than most, which allows you to see things many will not see.

Hindsight

The past is a strange experience when you think about it! We suppress things we did not like and pack them away in our memories until we forget. Even though we do not remember it, the trauma that we felt is still there. I have had to deal with many issues from the past to make space for new experiences in my mind. The weight of carrying around all this trauma can hold us back and because it is in our subconscience, we do not realize it. This happens with our parents, and I can remember things that happened when I was younger, but that I also forgot about. One example that stands out in my head was when tape recorders were popular and my father actually gave me one. He would always make mix tapes and was a big fan of all different kinds of music. One day my friends and I were recording down in the basement and we must have been about 8 or 9 years old I would guess. Well, we thought it was cool to say all kinds of swear words on the tape and were having a jolly ole time down there. Somehow, my uncle heard and he went to tell my mom about it. She spanked me and yelled at me about this and it traumatized me because I did not understand what was going on. I really feel this experience is what limited my career as a musician because I was so afraid to touch any equipment after that, and I could not understand why. I suppose I was too young to understand what the words actually meant, but my mom whooping me made me so afraid of anything related to that experience.

Of course the experience got buried, but I was still feeling the weight of it and I could not remember why. One day I was meditating and this vision of that situation came up in my head. I started to cry again and I felt that now was the time to do something about it. This actually happened when I was in my 30's so it was quite some time after the actual situation happened. What do most people do in this situation? What would you do in such a situation? I decided to forgive my mom and the only way I could do that was to call her and mention it.

When I called her and reminded her about that day, for her it was a vague memory. She was a young mom and probably just reacted the best way she knew how. She also mentioned that she did not remember the details, but she apologized for it and said she was sorry. This was such a huge weight off of my shoulders and actually freed up a bit of mental space. I was in a band in school, but could not get motivated enough to continue even though I really enjoyed being in the band. Once I was able to deal with this situation and forgive her, I was able to get back to music and I started djing at the only night club in Longyearbyen called Huset.

If you look closer at your feelings, then everything will eventually come back. It is just buried there and sometimes it is good to deal with these issues. The past is not always a sign of the future, but patterns should be observed and planned for. We only have this moment when you truly think about it! Tomorrow is never promised, and the past is already history. Being present is a skill that requires much discipline and skill to master. It is way too easy these days to multitask, but is it as productive as we think? I find it annoying when I am speaking with others, and they are busy with their phones. There is a vast difference between hearing someone speak and listening to that person. Listening is an active process, whereas hearing is more passive. The goal is to be present and aware when dealing with others, and this awareness will take you to the next level.

Stay Humble

I always strive to stay humble and not let anything that I have done go to my head. When you think about how many others have contributed to us being at this point in our lives, I could have never done this all alone. Why should I feel so proud and allow my ego to get the best of me during these experiences? Take the good with the bad, do the best you can, and then come back and do it all over again tomorrow. Learning from the mistakes and keep moving forwards have been my greatest lessons learned from this process. My goal has always been to get better and compete only against myself. I remember some of the people my father used to hang around and how he treated his guests. Even if he did not like someone, he was a great entertainer and always had an open door for all. My father was one of the most humble people I ever knew and he was great at reading people. My mother is also quite a humble lady and I believe that being humble runs in my family. My parents were conservative and would take us shopping at the thrift shop instead of buying us the latest fashions. I am really thankful for my family and also strive to be humble daily.

CONCLUSION

_____

In the end, the formula for achieving success is not all that complicated and is within grasp. Decide what you want, grow the desire in yourself like a huge bonfire, and then go after it with everything you have.

By following these principles:

1. The Sky's the Limit
2. Make Your Decision
3. Little By Little
4. The Impossible Is Possible
5. The Buck Stops Here
6. Be Present
7. Take A Chance
8. Words Are Things
9. Never Stop Learning
10. Learn From Failure

I hope that you are able to solve problems, overcome frustrations, develop patience, boost self-esteem, and improve yourself as a person. success will come and you will improve the overall quality of your life.

I did not know about these before I started up with Polar Permaculture on Svalbard, and I wish I would have known about them before as it would have saved me plenty of time and heartache.

You now have all you need to move forward and achieve all

you desire. By following these steps laid out here in this book, you should now be ready to face your future and shape your destiny.

Keep in touch and let me know how you get on as I am rooting for you and wishing you all the best!

AUTHOR'S BACKGROUND

My Story

Without a purpose, things will never make sense and will be extremely challenging for you to accomplish the impossible. When you have passion, anything is possible! Life has more meaning when there is purpose, and I would recommend you invest the time in yourself to find your purpose. What would you do if you never had to worry about money? Where would you be if you could be anywhere you wanted to be in the world? I have asked myself these questions many times before finally figuring out the answer.

Culinary School

Many times, we are so consumed with buying, spending, or earning love and affection that we never stop to think what we really want. I remember after I finished culinary school at the Le Cordon bleu School in Pittsburgh, PA, that I worked two full-time jobs and would not have much time to reflect on what my purpose was. A typical day for me was to do two full-time jobs and then go back home to sleep for a few hours before doing it all over again, day after day. A better day for me would mean only working one full-time job and being off from the other one. This meant that I only had to be outside of my home for 9 hours before spending time with my family.

What made a perfect day was when the planets aligned, and I was free from both of my jobs. This rarely happened, but when it did, I used the time to catch up on much needed rest. What do you do when you work two full-time jobs just to make ends meet, and you live faraway from each job? Well, it would have been extremely difficult to drive home after each one and it would have used up a lot of petrol. So, instead, I drove to the other job and would rest in the car before beginning work. This gave me time to read and dream about all the places I wanted to go and things I wanted to do around the world.

Permaculture

I would read Permaculture magazines and enjoyed reading Backwoods home magazines about being self-sufficient. How did people do that? I would wonder when reading as if I was reading some science fiction about some conceptual universe in the distant future. The ad would list courses that were available, for example, in Brazil to learn more about Permaculture and sustainability, and that they were two weeks long.

How did people have time to do those types of projects? I would ponder, as I was already working 16 to 18 hours per day and had no more time to spare. Not only that, but after working 16 to 18 hours a day as a chef in a private club and overnight at a bakery, I also had to help my ex-wife with household chores and our first-born child.

My Family

I was extremely young and naïve, so of course I married at 19 and had our son Amir to raise. It's funny, because as I am writing this, today is Amir's 22nd birthday. I was younger than he is now when I had him, but I am so grateful that he is in my life. Our children teach us more than we could ever teach them, and I am still learning from my children every day without fail. I met my son's mother while studying a year abroad in Malaysia in 1997. It was such an amazing experience for me, and I can remember wanting to see the world for as long as I can remember. In my high school classroom, I can remember a huge world map hanging in the room's front, and me always being distracted by it.

The teacher would speak and drone on, meanwhile I would only glance at the map and imagine what people were doing in each of those places and distant lands. That teacher asked what I wanted to do when I finished school and I said I wanted to travel the world. He recommended against it and suggested that I prepare for college, but there was nothing more that I wanted to do but travel. That was my passion. It is what consumed my thoughts most days during that time. I have always been around international groups and I grew up in a multicultural family. My mother is mixed with Native American and African American. My father is mixed with Slovenian and French blood. Not only that, but after my parents got divorced, my mother married an Italian man, and he added those cultural aspects and traditions to our family.

My Chef Heroes

Many Americans eat ham, turkey and bread stuffing for Thanksgiving and Christmas, but not in our house. We would eat seafood soup, fried calamari (squid), and octopus' salad. I grew up in such a foodie family without even realizing it, as my grandmother and mother are both foodies. I can remember going to the market with my grandmother when I was a child and getting live chickens slaughtered. It was fresh and so local, but then, of course, it was no longer possible because of regulations. My grandmother grew up in the south, and she loves fish. Not just any fish, but only fresh fish is good enough for her. My mom has always had a garden and would shop for her food daily from the farmer's market.

In Cleveland, Ohio, almost the midwest in the US, you have one of the most foodie and international selections I have experienced in the world. People who migrated there were segregated and formed their own neighborhoods. You have Little Italy, for example, where you find many Italian bakeries and shops. And where we grew up on the west side, there were many Spanish-speaking people around. I wish now I would have focused more on learning the language, but I was more concerned with eating the food. My stepfather would make my lunches for school, and it was embarrassing for me. Because all the other children in class would have perfect white bread squares with peanut butter and jelly, whereas my lunch consisted of fresh baked dark bread from the local bakery chock full of Mortadella from the local butcher, wrapped in simple brown paper. I felt so embarrassed to eat this sandwich and would usually throw it away out of fear that I would be mocked by my peers.

I remember going with my stepfather to the bakery, seeing the steam rising from the bread as the baker took it out of the oven. The baker spoke Spanish and my stepfather would speak a mix of Spanish/Italian in return before they both broke out in laughter at something one of them had said. I didn't understand a word of what they were saying, but I could tell that they both were having a great time. The situation at the butcher was remarkably the same as the interaction in the bakery, and the vivid memory of the butcher placing a huge chunk of meat on the meat slicer to cut and fill my stepfather's order. I remember looking at all the different labels and pronouncing them in my head, imagining what the name meant. The one that stood out the most to me was Mortadella, and it appeared to be my step-father's favorite.

He made my lunch and used extra virgin olive oil on the bread. Then he would put about four to five slices of Mortadella on thick slices of the round loaf of fresh bread. I also remember the smile on his face as he made lunch, but it was too early in the morning for me to understand what was going through his head. The way to school I would have to catch two buses and one metro train to get to school on the other side of town. The neighborhood where my school was located was an extremely sketchy place, but I never seemed to have trouble because I was "invisible". I would get to school and hear stories about kids who got robbed on their way to school, but most of those kids wore expensive clothes and flashy jewelry. I would shop at the thrift store and was doing it before it became cool and fashion-able. My parents divorced when I was young, so I went to three different high schools. I spent the first two years of high school in a small town living with my father. I had more friends there because I also went to the middle school there before attending high school, but once I moved with my mother to the inner city, I lost contact with most of those friends. My sister Heather and I spent my junior year at a high school on the west side of Cleveland. The boys would always chase her and usually try to use me to get closer to her.

Travels Abroad

I went to Martin L. King Jr. School on the east side of town for my senior year, and again had to make new friends. I didn't like John Marshall High School, which is why I wanted to try something different. MLK School was smaller, and I preferred that to the much larger Marshall high school. My stepfather was a concrete mason with a union job and did well for himself. He and my mom would ask me what I wanted to do after high school, and I said I wanted to travel the world. I truly wanted to go to the African continent and explore those nations, but my African friends advised against it and said that life in Africa would be difficult for me. I suppose it had to do with the fact that I was so innocent and naïve, but I didn't care and had to go somewhere. They suggested I go to Malaysia, because they also had friends there at a university that could assist me.

So, I applied to the International Islamic University of Malaysia (IIUM) and got accepted into the accounting program. My father, Larry, was quite happy about it and he even gave me $5000 dollars to assist with the entire process. I was still asking my parents for everything and was not independent yet. I was a momma's boy and would probably have been living with my mom until I was 40 years old had I not left the country. After receiving my acceptance letter, I prepared for my new adventure in the Far East. I remember packing four large suitcases before my travels with things that only a person from the US would think to pack. Why did I need to take 10 bottles of mouthwash? Did I really need so many clothes with me? I can remember how my friend from Uganda looked at me when I showed up at the University with these four enormous suitcases. He rolled his eyes.

My Passion for Malaysia

These students barely had one medium size bag that they

traveled with, yet I showed up with enough stuff for my whole dorm. The experience in Malaysia really taught me about passion and continued to develop my sense of adventure and flavors. My fondest memory of that experience is how popular street food is there and for good reason. People love to eat and the most common greeting, "sudah makan" literally means have you eaten. They don't ask how you are, or how your life is. They only want to know if you have had something to eat. The variety of food in Malaysia is phenomenal, being that there are three dominant cultures mixing there.

They have many Malay, Chinese, and Indian people, and all of them are so proud of their food. I was so surprised to find people there with carts of fresh fruit just standing near the road and selling the fresh cut, truly "fresh". That would have never happened in Ohio in a million years, and by the time you would have permission to do something like that, you would have been old. The people there were pleasant and friendly, as the major boost for the economy was tourism. My years in Malaysia shaped who I am as a person and further developed my food experiences. It also resulted in my first marriage and gave me three beautiful children: Amir, Alif, and Laila. I have drawn the passion I have felt to do what I have done from my experience as a father and the need to provide for my family.

Dealing with Racism

I can remember living in Cleveland, OH in the US and never feeling like I belonged there or fit in. The energy required to deal with race issues in the States is exhausting, and I believe it is much more complicated for multiracial people. Cleveland is one of the most racist places I have ever lived in the world, but it was impossible for me to understand this when I was growing up there. I will never understand why the color of someone's skin is so important to any decision that is made there, but it most definitely is an issue. This was always a turnoff for me, and my eyes opened when I left to see the world. Around the world, people seem to be divided more by language and culture, but not in the States. The most important ingredient is the color of your skin, and then they decide. It was such a liberating experience to free up all this energy that was used to deal with racism and put it into more productive areas of my life. I first arrived in Svalbard in 2007 as part of a team working on chartered Russian research vessels for expedition companies. I met my second wife Elena there and we have a wonderful daughter, Vlasa, together.

The three of us have moved down from Svalbard to Lofoten in Norway. Everything in my life has led up to this moment of me reaching the "northernmost" town in the world, Longyearbyen. To get here, I had to make an important choice between two options that were presented to me by my mom and stepfather. My education experience in Malaysia did not go according to plan. I would not be still long enough to do the studies required to become an accountant. I soon dropped out of that program and was experiencing life. I found a part-time job as a server in a Turkish restaurant in Kuala Lumpur, Malaysia. This was back in 1997, and the chefs still smoked in the kitchen. I remember standing in the restaurant and looking at them, laughing and having so much fun in the kitchen. As a server, it was important to be attentive, professional, and quiet. The total opposite of what I saw the chefs doing in the kitchen and I wanted in on that mischief. It was a great experience in Malaysia. I had already been there for around 11 months, and my mother grew concerned.

Time to Go Home

My mother called me one day, and we had a serious conversation about how things were and what I was doing there. I finally told her I quit school, which I had kept a secret from my parents out of shame. She then instructed me I should return home because if I was only working there, it did not seem enough of a reason to remain. Being the momma's boy, I respected her decision and promptly bought a ticket home. Part of me was homesick, and that she had said perhaps I was relieved by her directions. Once I made it back home, I took a much-needed break and just reacclimated myself to the Midwestern climate after being in a tropical paradise for almost a year.

My parents voiced concern about my next moves and my mom asked me what I wanted to do? They presented me with two choices, and that shaped my future. The first option was to join the union and get a construction job like my stepfather. He was a well-respected journeyman and could have secured me a well-paid job with his company. The second option was to go to culinary school in Pittsburgh, Pennsylvania and become a chef. This decision was straightforward for me because I do not enjoy working outside in the summer heat. That was the primary season for the construction workers, and then they usually get laid off in the winter. I had had so many chefs around me that the thought of me becoming a chef came naturally. My grandmother is the best chef I know, and my mom is a close second.

Time to Go to School

I began preparing to go east to study and get experience. Culinary school was amazing, and I met so many interesting people. I remember when we first started school, they issued us our uniforms; we went to the nightclub and wore our chef uniforms. It was so impulsive and truly a gamble that paid off. We were the heroes of the night, and everyone gave us respect. I also remember slacking off in the pastry part of the program because my classmate and I had both decided that we wanted to be chefs and did not need to learn the art of pastry. I regret that now and wish I would have given the pastry program more attention and respect. We did enough to pass, but it is strange how we think we know something at a moment and then totally find ourselves in an opposite situation later. Now I feel that pastry and baking is my favorite part about being a chef, and I cannot think of anything better than fresh baked bread. Of course, school only gives the basics, and it is still necessary to gain experience from years of hard work and sacrifice. My first experience after school was working as a chef in a private club inside the tallest building in the city. This club was frequented by the "upper echelon" of the city, and there is no way I would have been able to have access to these folks if I was not working there.

My First Mentor

My favorite mentor found me at this club and "saw" something in me. Reverend Paul was the first person who stoked my fires of passion for business and being a chef. He would ask me important questions that have led me on a journey around the world. Not only would he encourage me to think bigger, but he also gave me opportunities to cater for events at his church and earn money. I would not be where I am today if it was not for him guiding me during the early stages of my career. He also helped me develop my imagination and to visualize what I wanted to do and have. After I started catering for his church groups, I imagined myself as a business owner. No longer did I only see myself as a cook at a restaurant. I desired to have my very own business, and this created a passion in me that drove me forward.

Finding my Purpose

Having a purpose is necessary to achieve the impossible and to build up the patience required to move forwards. Are you interested in building up your dream or are you going to help build up someone else's dream is a question I would always ask myself? It is also possible to help someone else build their dream while building up your own dream, but that requires laser guided focus and keen listening skills. Many times in life, we have different people saying what we should do, and we usually try to accommodate such wishes when we are younger. As a child, it is important to seek acceptance of authority figures to feel safe and appreciated. This can and often stunts our developing passion and operating more from a position of security. How will my parents feel about me becoming an artist? It might not be so welcoming if you are from a family of doctors or lawyers, for example. Many times, we seek to please others at the expense of our purpose and skills.

Being a chef and working with food came naturally because of my background, but for many years I had ignored or neglected it because of pressure to get a college degree and be something that I was not. I have nothing against getting a university degree, but it is not for everyone. I feel that as I was growing up, the pressure to get a degree was immense and that other options were not presented equally. There was a career fair at the high school that I attended and luckily, I could connect with the culinary school and find out more information about it. Even as I spoke with the representative, I felt good about the place, however my mind got in the way and caused distractions. I attended university a few times, and the results ended up the same. It was uncomfortable for me; it was not a fit. Therefore, I think it came down to two choices for me regarding where I wanted to focus my energy towards a career: work as a construction worker with the union like my stepfather or to go to culinary school. The universe was slowly pushing me towards my destiny, and all I had to do was get out of my own way.

Once I signed up for culinary school, I felt a new purpose in my life and finally felt home in what I needed to do. As I prepared to attend school, there were many things to pack and think about. I would go alone to Pittsburgh, but after spending a year in Malaysia, this would be a piece of cake. I arrived at the Le Cordon Bleu School that was at the time called Pennsylvania Culinary and fell right into place.

Support from My Chefs

My chef stood up for me because, of course, I was there to be a student, but I learned a valuable lesson that day. The lesson is that we must always be careful how we treat others and deal with people. I did not know that this chef would go back to my school with a complaint like that and it made me realize how everything is connected and how important it is to maintain a positive reputation. My purpose at this point was to become a chef, and the way to do that was to finish school and get as much experience as possible.

I was not thinking about the lessons I have learned from my grandmother or my mother at this point. In my mind, I still looked down on these experiences and considered the chefs I met at school to be "real chefs". The illusion that I would only learn from pro chefs consumed me for the early part of my career. After school, I worked with a talented chef named Jim.

He taught me so many important things and I consider him a philosopher's chef because he had so much wisdom outside of cooking. He was a superb chef, but his focus was not on himself, and he was more concerned with making more brilliant chefs. He once told me that the secret to being a skilled chef is not how much you can do or accomplish, but how much you can get others to do and accomplish.

He would also push us to be the best and to be the fastest chefs that have ever existed in the world. Not only that, but we needed to deliver the highest quality products to our guests and customers. I would have to say that Chef Jim had the greatest impact on my career and my thoughts towards being a chef. He further developed my purpose and solidified what it meant for me to be a chef. I messaged him a few times, and he was happy to hear from me, and I told him I am still his number one fan until today.